born again, now as myself

poems

Su Van Gelder

new words {press}
A TRANS* & GENDER-EXPANSIVE POETRY PRESS

new words {press}
6030 Putnam Ave., New York, NY 11385
www.newwordspress.com | @newwordspress

new words {press} is a sponsored project of Fractured Atlas, a non-profit arts service organization with a mission of elevating emerging and established trans* and gender-expansive poetic voices, to build community, and share knowledge.

ISBN: 979-8-9903488-5-1

Cover design by Jackson C. Smith
Typesetting by new words {press}

Printed in the United States of America

For my Chumby Partner and our beloved Zeppy cat,
may she rest in eternal sunshine.

The love and warmth you give me is undying, and my heart is yours, com-
pletely.

Table of Contents

I. Metamorphoses

breaking a thing

—After *Special Problems in Vocabulary* by Tony Hoagland

in the time between caterpillar
and blooming lepidoptera
there is only goop.

nothing but potential energy
and instinct, all soupy and
stewed together inside a chrysalis.

now, in the times when I cry
standing in front of the
supermarket Hanukkah display,

when nighttime scoops out my
coping mechanisms with a
plastic serving spoon,

I remember the luna moth, perched
on the same wood panel of the garage,
called back each year by that ancestral imperative.

Somehow through generations, through
the process of liquifying one's entire existence,
there's the promise of wings when the chrysalis breaks.

the Leaving Day

Love, no longer, is a primary source.
Our lips meet only transitively,
at the top of the cat's head or
the mouth of the bong.

Conversation values simplicity over substance.
Brevity, my worst nightmare,
achilles heel, has
made itself your champion.

Maybe, in some dystopian dream we are
perfect complements,
but in the Here & Now
we are abstinent of each other.

These are not the wasted years.
We are not completed stories.
This, I promise, is the breaking
of waves, the future we have made—

the incarnation of my happiness.

Picking up old hobbies

$75 and a penchant for bargaining
is all you need to buy a used trombone
in Manchester Center, VT.

Now, the Winter can get so warm
around here that it's better to leave
your jacket in the car and just wear the flannel.

This is one of those transient towns,
the meeting and leaving place of
old friends, the center of self-reflection.

Sometimes, I still buy things I don't want rather
than suffer the guilt of leaving empty-handed.
Lately, I'm always carrying something.

Martin's watchful eye

yesterday We woke up hand-in-hand
eyes soft shut to the warmth of morning
and laughed. Friendship forged eternal,
serotonin sickness siblings.

This is the aftermath of a new childhood
home, burned and re-built
into something charitable.

Hope, here, is a 4-letter lovesong,
a Planned Parenthood poster, a bug on
the railing, a handprint in
a notebook, a moment

in our history

XO

I must have been absent on the day where
        we all found the fountain of youth,
        ran naked through the garden,
        touched all the soft parts.

I missed the Ocean melody in the morning haze
        where we breathed each other in
        haled through poorly rolled joints,
        tangled up our stomachs,
        cried in the tenderness.

I was late to the party where we got drunk enough
        for messy lips and slow fingers,
        skin on skin on skin on skin on skin
        desperate and cinematic
        and oh so unspeakably lovely.

I missed the impressionism and the album of the year
        and the fingers in the mouth...

XX (Motherhood)

My body is sour today.
The flavor of my image
so unpleasant that my eyes
pucker and wince. Bitter,
is how it tastes to put on
six shirts before settling.

On the best days my soul
is sweet, bones twine-wrapped
in aromatics. Today my sage
and citrus peels are overcome
by the taste of tonic.

I watch a couple place
their baby in the backseat,
look at each other lovingly.
French vanilla, coffee, bergamot,
the mother turns and smiles at me.
Some days my body feels rotten.

Pesach and Past Selves

I have spent so much time in cars that I feel myself age in them
The quiet realization of a childhood behind me.
On the steering wheel my hands look like Mom's,
Passover matzo encased in cloth napkins.

I shed childhood like corduroy overalls—
things Dad wanted for me that I never understood.
Secrets I saved feel calcified now. Cigarettes I never told them about,
the dent in the bumper of my first car, tattoos I've hid
in rebellious places.

And already I've lived two lives, one in captivity
and one in defiance of my former self.

Adulthood is the first full inhale after a panic attack.
The first shower after a depressive episode.
The first day of being halfway content with the collection of grocery
lists and poorly done hobbies and life choices and drives to work
that make you a person.

and Here is where I judge my age.
Does my chest feel the same as it always has?

The empty feels different, though.
less substantial and more enduring,
a grief you've learned to live with.
Same eyes only older, same body only bigger, same child
but not a daughter.

A phantom pain, an empty chair at the Passover seder,
an adult, a fool, a reflection of a mother.

I killed something

and the ghost in the house refuses to pass on.
        When I feel it pass through me   I shudder.

It's always lurking somewhere close—
        in the armchair   in the quiet
        during breakfast   while we distract ourselves

It's clasping its hands in my stomach,
        grinding its teeth   in my throat.

We have no spells or ceremonies to evict it, it rots
        the boards between us   as long as the pullout bed
stays out,   until we say goodbye,   for as long as it takes

to feel lucid again.

Maybe just for a moment   I could possess that spirit
        and I could rest   from outside of myself.

acid sunset

the world is expanding faster than it can carry me,
and I race to catch up with her. If I put enough weight
                              on my toes

I can feel   the gravity change,
          I can feel myself   swell   with the sky.
there is an ecosystem in the railing water,
    swallowed now by the fuchsia reflection and   oh   oh wow
the clouds!   they form a world and if I could just
              put enough   weight on my toes
          I could join them, I could join them! I could be a part of the
sky and oh
ah,
          a dr
                    a dragon?
                         no, a dragon!

          luck, my friend, floats me a companion to protect the house
he's slender and gentle   his nose looks like my first dog's nose
and
          there's the smoke!
                              trailing up and off and if if I could   I
really think I could

          put enough weight   on   on my toes   to drift
                    into the fuchsia   trail off
into the rolling, the churning, the ocean clouds   if I never close my
eyes, never   close   never close

              never close   my eyes
              I could float off.

It'll be a month tomorrow.

The morning was long today. I was
slow to rise and am worse for it.
My chest is a cavity where something's decaying,
every song on my 'Best of the Decade' playlist
drills deeper to the root.

It has nothing to do with seeing your ring on the bathroom sink this
morning.
That doesn't have to do with any of this.

I grip yesterday's snow in my fist.
Nevermind the way it burns my palm, I
have to know how long it takes to melt completely.
Something about mind over matter,
or persistence, or the
price of destroying something.

It has nothing to do with seeing your ring on the bathroom sink this
morning.
I haven't worn mine in weeks.

I notice my friend's bumper stickers, my
eyes searchlights for neurons. I can't
stop thinking about holding him. Nothing
like sex, only safe in the sense that
I'd like to cry into him and kiss his tattoos—
shameful, semi-artistic and disgusting.
He looks like all my monochrome dreams
and I just want to sleep in him for a while.

It has nothing to do with seeing your ring on the bathroom sink this
morning.
I promise, I felt nothing.

It'll be a week tomorrow

It still feels wrong to come home
to nothing.   No one
to greet us as we take off our shoes,
no one to lift their head from the couch
and bid us welcome   with a blink,
beep, yawn & stretch-out,   your paw beckoning
"come, sit. love me more."

You left on a sunbeam, hung back
to watch us for an evening and
meet us   in our dreams.
For the first time in my life I could
recognize the face in the full moon
I'd know your peaceful gaze and   yellow-olive eyes anywhere,
through darkness, an eclipse, an old moment of deja vu,
even my real and imagined faults.
And you'll know me
every time.

Today I laid in your favorite spot
in the sun, looked to the door with the hope
you would join me. I keep wondering when
all this goes away, when   life without you feels full again.

It's been more than a year without my uterus
and close to four without birth control pills,
and I still   jolt myself up at the edge
of sleep with the thought I forgot my medication.
Why do I do that? Those times are   long gone.
I guess there are things the spirit   can't release,
things the body remembers   forever.
Kinds of love that the heart goes on knowing,
eternally

We love you, Zeppy.

16

Effigy

I built an effigy of myself. She looms,
glares with expectant eyes. When I'm quiet she speaks to me,
asks all the impossible questions.

I built it so long ago I don't recognize her as myself.
I show her my accomplishments and she doesn't respond.
I beg her for providence and she remains, unwavering.

I tear out her teeth with vengeful fingers
I have to know if she bleeds like me,
if we have congruent nightmares,
if her tongue is the strongest muscle in her body.

When the house was bigger I kept an altar for her.
In the confines of the insect-ridden apartment,
I trip over her feet,
scrape my knees for her.
By now I have forgotten every prayer I wrote in her name.

At night, her silhouette commands the dark.
Her questions are eternal, insistent.
My prayers are forgotten, and in their place a mantra.

Burn her, burn her, burn her.

Idolatry

the receptionist here calls me "girlfriend!"
because (I'm guessing) the tits give something away
that the hairy legs and monstrousness couldn't obscure.
this thought makes my brain convulse,
thrash about and throw the sweaty sheets
off me as I untangle from nightmares and diction.
Each morning is a new day for penance, castigation
through repeated dressing and undressing, misgenderings
by baristas, and of course,
the unceasing affliction of existing as myself.

I'm ready to return now
to the place of femicide and covered mirrors
and erect a monument there.
Something unmistakably androgyne
shapely and formless, called by every name
and known only by one, symbolizing all
bodies and absolutely nothing at all. I'm
ready to call out now
to every aura and entity as yet unseen
and aid them in pilgrimage to our Idols.
Laughing and rolling and dancing in
reverence of these bodies, in defiance
of our old names, in celebration of
our survival.

I'm ready to be born again,
now as myself. True and fluid form,
sustained by love, anger, and T4T,
loyal only to chosen family and
sex, drugs, and rock & roll.
monstrous, joyous, Trans, unfathomable...
whatever, really. I am.

II. Reflexions

Hospital//Cardinal

Hospital

While I shower, he leaves for the hospital.
I step out dripping, naked, angry
like this baby photo of me where I'm purple and screaming...

I'm checking myself into the hospital, he says.
Doesn't want to be a problem to me anymore.
I worry if they've taken a mask for the wildfire smoke descending
from the North. If he packed anything for himself. If I'll make it to
office hours for statistics tonight. If partners are supposed to visit their
lovers in the mental hospital.
How long do these things usually take?

Cardinal

They always say "it's not your fault" as if
the source of pain is singular. Has anyone
ever killed themselves for just *one* reason?
No use pondering it now. I'll just collect
the anecdotal evidence when I'm dead.
We'll all sit, together, AA meeting style,
a bunch of birds lamenting their life and
death. Cardinals. All of us, perched outside
windows of white people who think we
mean something. Find the spirits
of your dead relatives elsewhere, we're busy
standing sentry at the windows of people
crying in their bath towel, fresh out the womb
of the shower and into the world of
smoke.

Maybe the hospital isn't a bad idea. Maybe
everything *is* bad. But hey look,
there's cardinals right outside the window…

Recovery, one day at a time

You can't tell me how to grieve
if you've never given someone your charity
only for them to squish it in their fist,
the rotted fruits of your labor.

Here are some things I know about compassion:

Sometimes what is mutual isn't equal.
Love, for example.

'What you give' and 'what you get' are
trains moving in opposite directions,
but you're going to chase them both
anyway.

When you're sick, sympathy and chicken ramen
taste nearly identical.

I say these things because sometimes people say
"I love you more than anything"

and they really mean
"I need you to survive"

and sometimes people say
"I need you to survive"

when they really mean
"Your love is only worthwhile when it's useful to me."

There will be times when "I love you" is
nothing more than eyewitness testimony

when the pendulum hangs limp with answers
but we have to trust that love will swing back,
knock us over clumsily and catch us, laughing.

Otherwise, what is empathy but a gateway drug to loss?

last night home

the water heater rumbles and hums
in perpetuity. Unchanging,
it never asks about the things I hide.

the off-white noise drowns out
everything except the inner flows.
blood in the carotid, air in the chamber,

guilt on the mind.

VACANCY

the mouth wears a neon vacancy sign.   it is less an invitation for
occupants, and more a proclamation of self.   sleep is suggested by
the incessant buzzing of the neon tubes
but there is no one to occupy the beds.   the body is a place
for things to visit,   but never stay.
the groundskeeper is home sick for days at a time.
beds stay unmade   lights stay out   lungs are boarded shut.
the missing guests speculate the secrets hidden in the sternum.
someone buried the bones beneath the floorboards long ago
          and the dust calls   for someone else to unearth them.
behind the teeth of heavy curtains lies the revolting truth
          of solitude.   sun-faded and crying, the
          NO TRESPASSING   sign wishes for someone to
disobey it   and break the curse of lonesome.
          through the cracks in the skin of the parking lot   the ferns
arrive and die.   the melancholy of this place is housed in everything
avoided, untouched,   and   forgotten.   a house for anyone
but a home for no one   too much charity has made this place
decrepit   has left this body empty.   VACANCY
          screams the buzzing,   but the body   chases away
the guests.

Infinitive

on the walk back from the communal cry session
they held downtown I pause to rest

outside the house with the newest iteration of the pride flag,
identity after identity mashed together to fit

inside one rectangle.

the fireflies flash on and off with manic ignorance
which I string together in my witch brain to mean

they are guiding me somewhere, or they have brought me here.
I pluck off my first black raspberry of the season, too sweet

for today.

in a few steps the canopy clears to reveal the Ithaca sky at dusk
an old friend come out to comfort

me. nights like this I'd sit out with Jaco and joke
our genders into existence, too naive

to realize we were already there.

when the sky ran pink and blue and white we'd sound the alarm
THE SKY IS TRANS (attachments: 4 photos) to tell

each other *the world is with us*, if only for the half hour before dark.
Tonight I screamed beneath a red sharpie sign too small

to touch the cisgender psyche.

on this day where not enough feels like nothing at all
one trans kid found me in the crowd to ask

if they could take a picture of my sign. The whole walk
back I think about this kid, too beautiful

and bright and brilliant for a world built to extinguish them

but right now, the sky glows queer and triumphant,
one endless stretch of infinitive transness too powerful

to capture or quantify. Right now,
the sky is Trans, I am Trans, and together

we might make a sharpie sign big enough to stretch over the whole
horizon,

the world is with us.

Urban Foraging

Once I learned the names
of the plants that could heal and feed,
that was the end. Every peripheral leaf was someone
that I had to introduce.

That's mint, I know her from the square stem.
Garlic Mustard?
Yeah, I know them.
Nosy, invasive, drowning everyone out…

Outside of work
there's treasure in the parking lot,
the barely-soil gravel meridians.
Dandelion, plantain, cleavers.

There's good medicine
if you know where to look. A patch of empty shooters
is growing outside of the AA building
and might be ready for harvest soon.

Every urban foraging guide gives helpful warnings:
Don't gather where pesticides are sprayed. Don't harvest by roadsides.
Be mindful of what you put in your body.
I hear that in cities all the sacred spaces are coated in chemicals.

I used to be so fearless with the pricker-bushes,
pushing my soft child arms
into the thicket for the best blackberries.
Now I'm more careless than brave

kicking up used needles
nestled in the deadnettles,
catching my sleeves
on brambles that I failed to notice.

Mom handed me down her copy of *Stalking the Wild Asparagus*
and I reward her with a phone call.

Regale her of my bounty. This time,
lemon balm, turkey tail, ramps.

She says that book is actually so sad,
an old resource for a potential runaway.
I remind her of the medicinal plants pamphlet I memorized,
the night She and Dad sat me down and explained

why I should never run away.
And that's all behind us now.

A MAJOR PAIN IN THE EAR//a minor pain in the ear

A MAJOR PAIN IN THE EAR

it's all knots,
the narratives, the stomach pains,
the reasons for it all.
in the center of the tangled   there are teeth,
grinding their way through the fray,
biting off   just more than they can chew.
every bit I unravel is another fresh scab I pick open.
subconsciously   I'm tearing, scratching
as if comfort comes from perpetual motion.
there's a familiar discomfort to this entanglement.
I know all the methods of organization,
how they work,   where they sting,   all the side effects
I keep untangling
until my nails peel back.
one undone and another's formed, one bone mended
and another broken. and still,
in the endless futility,
there's an impulse   that drives me on,
that blisters my fingers,

that finds a knot for me to tie
just so I can undo it again.

a minor pain in the ear

little more than two years
and I've still got this itch in my ear,
an occasionally incessant whisper
barely discernible from
moral compass or conscience.

One of the tricks of the trade,
just keep your back bent
and then the pain is always your fault
and fixable.
Works for me, maybe half the time
at least.

Do you ever get spooked by it?
The sheer size of everything?

I'm so terrified to catch a glimpse through a kitchen window
to steal a moment from someone else's story

all because my errant eyes happened to
catch them at the breakfast table.

Or truthfully, selfishly, I'm
panic-stricken
with the thought
that I'm small enough to exist
in

fifty thousand kitchen windows,
half-remembered childhood dreams,
uncomfortable glances, drunk girl snapchats,
foolish choices and life stories,

and they
(and I)
won't remember
a single thing.

On the outskirts of Voyeurism

As part of my journey of being
okay with "good enough"
I learn to be
satisfied
with existing as a side character.

We forget the value of the faceless figures
that fill the background of dreams, bystanders
that incite pure fear
when stepping out in a new and questionable haircut,
nameless drivers to scream our daily frustrations at
while stuck on the Garden State Parkway.

We're all a part of someone's sexual fantasy,
if not the sweaty locker room heartthrob
then at least the unwitting bystander trying to enjoy
a light lunch while a young woman squirms
in her vibrating panties,
practically sick with ecstasy and shame.

What a strange honor, to be included
in one's intimacy and go about life
none-the-wiser. A background actor in
a wet dream, just necessary enough to live
in the deep subconscious of every person
to ever forget my face.

espolón* in my side

in no simple terms can I justify to you
the long-forgotten companion in our freezer,
Scooby, beloved boy and last living rodent
      (As of July 20, 2022) of the 4-man rat pack.

only now can I bring myself to rise from the kitchen floor
and gather the penance bread from the oven,
made with malice and the wrong kind of baking powder/soda
(it's absolutely scorched to ruin)

I thought the predictive dreams had gone.

You stay home with the cat— I insist.
I barrel towards the operating table and still,
there's something wrong
I have been *so patient*
               so pained

Still I have been found wanting.

If you could only harvest empathy
perhaps I could teach you to reap and sow— but nevermind.
I think it's too cold to grow where you're living
It's too harsh to thrive where I'm headed.

Wishful thinking has fattened me dumb and dull
and I had such high hopes for dessert.
      I had such splendid plans for the next harvest,

but that's all gone from me now.

Spanish: (n.) spur

not the magnum opus

The proverbial "they" have ordered us inside.
There has to be more to it.
Nothing conspiratorial,
       no second coming of Christ
       or dumping microchips in the water supply
       just
whispered anxieties over breakfast.

The proverbial "they" say that if
you leave a monkey with a typewriter for long enough,
it'll write Shakespeare.
I, defective specimen, stare at my typewriter
until it rusts. I could be left alone until
fists become stones
bones become anchors
teeth become leaves.
       Still, I won't write the next miracle into existence.

The proverbial "they" has kept me confined and called it Eden.
No thanks to them, I say.
What good have they done me? I say.
I, experimental failure, stare at the apples
until the forbidden fruit shrivels away with age.
I could be left alone until
         the next paper pandemic
         the next coming of "they"
         the next birth of a world.
Still, I wouldn't eat from that tree.

       Still, I won't write anyone's scripture.

To put it simply,

last night I was ready to kill myself
and today I walked outside
gasped as I nearly stepped on a pavement worm

>   it might not know it, but I do, that
>   nothing that worked so tirelessly to save
>   itself from drowning deserves to be crushed

by the great boot from above.

(for Gabriel and Me)

The Prison of Survival

Today I spit right in the eye of God
as I ruminate on how to remove my uterus
and still retain

                     my homosapien right to cum.

Even more than usual, I'm nauseated
by the curse of femininity. A rabbit's curse, really,
to be treated with kindness in exchange for
soft bodies and glassy, scared eyes
And devoured the moment they turn their back.

The world is so much simpler and deadly when you're beautiful
                     and fate won't let me forget it.

I pitch up my voice at the cashier
easy as dislocating a joint   and setting it back in place.
Just as painful as responding to "Thank you, ma'am"
with nothing more than
                 "You're welcome."

My partner says that "People do what's easy to survive."
Easy,   easy as
reclining back on a bed of nails. A rabbit's curse, truly,
to be born inevitable prey and aspire to something different.
Not predatory, really
                 something rabid, rather?
And be put down the moment they announce themselves,
frothing, disoriented, and possibly deranged.

Today I spit straight up at the eye of God
dancing my dress into pentagrams and screaming
"I'm not man nor woman, and I am free from all laws!"

before gravity laughed my spit
back down into
my right
eye.

About The Author

Su Van Gelder is a queer-nonbinary poet, punk, and public health professional. Su received their BA in Culture & Communication from Ithaca College in 2020 and is currently working on a Master of Public Health in LGBTQ health at Rutgers University. As an undergraduate they were an active participant in the Spit That! spoken word poetry club as a general body member, Communications Coordinator, and finally Co-president. After opening for Neil Hilborn in Ithaca in 2019 and being selected as a finalist for the 2020 Iowa Review Poetry Award, they thought "Hell, I might be pretty good at this poetry thing." Since then, Su has been published in Beyond Queer Words, Reservoir Road Literary Review, SIXFOLD, and others. Outside of poetry, Su is an avid forager of edible plants and mushrooms, advocate for the QT+ community, incredible singer, humble-bragger, and all-around rockstar. This is Su's first book, and they are tremendously thankful for every reader, editor, publisher, and muse that made it possible.

About nw{p}

new words {press} is a non-profit poetry press publishing trans* & gender-expansive poets & hybrid writers.

support our efforts & the incredible writers we publish. visit us at

newwordspress.com

new words {press}

A TRANS* & GENDER-EXPANSIVE POETRY PRESS

Aknowledgements

First Publication Credits:

"Effigy." *Beyond Queer Words*, Februrary 2023
"breaking a thing." *SIXFOLD*, Summer 2022.
"idolatry." *SIXFOLD*, Summer 2022.
"Not the Magnum Opus." *SIXFOLD*, Summer 2022.
"VACANCY." *SIXFOLD*, Summer 2022.
"The Prison of Survival." *Reservoir Road Literary Review, Issue 08*.